THE CHARM

&

THE DREAD

Author photograph by Clare Welsh
Book design by Rebecca Wolff

Published in the United States by

Fence Books
110 Union Street
Second Floor
Hudson NY 12534

www.fenceportal.org

This book was printed by Versa Press
and distributed by Small Press Distribution
and Consortium Book Sales and Distribution.

Library of Congress Cataloguing in Publication Data
Toscano, Rodrigo [1964–]
The Charm & The Dread / Rodrigo Toscano

Library of Congress Control Number: 2021947006
ISBN 13: 978-1-944380-22-9

First Edition
10 9 8 7 6 5 4 3 2

RODRIGO TOSCANO

FENCE BOOKS

HUDSON NY

Contents

The Charm & The Dread

A MEDITATION IN THE TIME OF COVID

Take a deep breath in.

Take a deep breath out.

In.

Out.

There is no past.

There is no future.

There is only now.

There is only now.

Trees . . . are hilarious.

Grass . . . is hilarious.

The charm of roots.

The charm of clouds.

The charm of that faucet that's leaking again.

A Dohblin ahccent (how'd the fock that get in hire?)

Take a deep breath in.

Deep breath out.

Welcome to China.

Floating flowers in air.

The crimson yellow of no past.

The charcoal pink of no future.

Trees don't select flight seats at the time of purchase.

Grass doesn't need to know the hotel check-out time.

Oceans.

Oceans.

Oceans.

Oceans.

Breathe in.

Hold your breath.

Don't let it out.

Hold your breath.

Sing "New York, New York" in your chest.

Knees clacking together.

Release your breath.

Welcome to Bourbon Street.

There is only now.

Ah-dohn-deh eh-stah lah cantina deh Tequila?

Oceans.

Oceans.

Oceans.

The charm of a medivac helicopter.

The dread of a failed meditation.

The charm of another ambulance.

The dread of a failed meditation.

The charm of a virus on your fingertip.

The dread of a failed meditation.

The charm of a curved graph line.

The dread of a failed meditation.

Take a deep breath in.

Deep breath out.

Two petals.

An emerald white of no past.

A lavender orange of no future.

There is only now.

Blue, with a hint of silver.

Oceans.

Oceans.

The last puddle on your street.

The power of a cat finding it.

The last flower of a hibiscus plant.

The power of a worm chomping it down.

That damn rooster again.

The rooster again.

The rooster.

Rooster.

Rue.

Stir.

Welcome to Antarctica.

Ah-dohn-deh eh-stah — *breathe in*.

Icebergs.

Icebergs.

Icebergs.

Nobody.

Nobody.

Nobody told you to stop breathing.

Nobody told you to *start* breathing.

Nobody told you — stop goofing.

Nobody told you to stop regarding that leaky faucet.

Droplets — one by one — is music.

Birds — one by one — is music.

The clouds are hamming it up.

Your heart it is hamming it up.

Your lungs are hamming it up.

Your belly is hamming it up.

Your tongue is hamming it up.

Your toes are hilarious.

Your toes have always been hilarious.

Night sky, stars.

Night sky, stars.

Night sky, stars.

Maskers

People will forget, or want to forget
All this rubbish of masks, all this haggling
The so-called "tough" non-masker, the said "weak"
You can see some here! young, at river's edge
Fully masked quartet, likely monster free
With shield and sword, phalanx facing the foe
Someone else's death — not their own, they stand
Stoutly defend their people — *all* people
While popping, or trying to pop, pink champagne
Spilling over muffled conversation
One springs up to take a gulp, six feet off
And here comes a fifth! black, bloody fanged mask
Completing the quintet, soon forgotten
Save for this sonnet straining against it

Miasma

And suddenly, the words are gone again
The globe's entire surface of meaning
Has been wiped clean, what lingers is absence
Tightly banded around your mouth and nose
Making its way to the next waiting spot
Procession in a cadence of silence
Choreography of the miasma
Something in the air, separate from the air
Something that can seize you, make you its own
Offer you to the spiky mothership
Intelligence of no intelligence
Impervious to all arts to name it
Though we name it, give it a million names
And witness a million names flicker out

Squander

Immersive fear, immersive confusion
As the sky goes from blue to red to black
Angry flies abuzz in weeds encroaching
A hunching, sprawling tree teeming with fruit
You pick one, one at a time, once a day
Peel the bitter harboring succulence
And ponder the squander of recourses
Of leadership, of coordination
Of disconnected care, entombed in pride
Told as a heroic tale to the serfs
Tending to the dry fields of denial
Immersive hope, immersive augury
Clouds bubbling up, air at a standstill shrieks
Flicker of the whole village, bat shit scattered

Coding

The Pandemic is no longer an external event, rather
it is an interiority in search of an externality.

The George Floyd protests are no longer an externality,
they are an internality seeking an externality.

Both the pandemic and the protests form a singularity;
the New Event, as a code, is seeking hosts.

I'm a host, you're a host, unshielded and waiting. Isolated,
we're all watching The Code do its thing. Symptoms vary.

Betimes

A RHAPSODY FOR ACTIVISTS

Betimes, you *stall*, and by stalling, *rocket*

Betimes, you're a dead-bored worker

Betimes, a devoted worker without deep purpose

Betimes, you're a thrill-seeking slacker

Betimes, a genius *co*-worker — without peers

You *chose* this, you chose dialectical wreck sensational

You pounce toward direct intents unknown

You've sloughed off crooked dick nationalism

You've blown up indolence (on some occasions, eloquence)

Who can Velcro on a plasticized red wig when you want it?

Who can supply you a bronze lion future beast of victory?

Betimes, you're a *pre*-pounce poet, posing as *pouncer*

Betimes, you're a *post-pounce* as twitchy twitch

Not whatever! *Never* whatever! But *this*:

You're a *Spectral* Socialist — savage

You're a *Spectral* Socialist — civilizer

You're a *Spectral* Socialist — dirt clod on diamond

Who can futurize "The People" without the trademark?

Who enacts fire canister hierarchical reform?

Betimes, you carouse, and by carousing, arouse

Betimes, you're a "hella" (as y'all say) cat with hiss *and* claws

Betimes, you're a devotee to love slamming you to the ground

Did you really *choose* this gem? Art thou chosen?

Are you ascending now towards free-floating domes in the sky?

Have you handily sloughed off sultry stance nationalism?

Betimes, nationalisms offer *services* — left *or* right

Betimes, *intra*-nationalisms show a way out — for a fee

Who can hyper-spatialize "The People" without coordinates?

Who enacts super symmetrical justice reform?

You're a *Spectral* Socialist — bit actor

You're a *Spectral* Socialist — stunt double

You're a *Spectral* Socialist — diamond fleck on demon dung

Betimes, you *rocket*, and by rocketing, *stall*

Betimes, you *stall*, and by stalling, *rocket*

Insurrectionary

The day to day existence of people
If that doesn't change, then what is all this?
These protests, these stances, rage, pieties
Passionate words, eloquent poetry
What's the use of any of it today
If tomorrow and many days to come
Aren't *shaped* differently, aren't *lived* differently
Which calls the question: what do people want?
What do they *want*, not just what they *don't* want
Let's list it, let's study the list closely
And before these items are pinned to life
Let's have *that* conversation: what is life?
What kinds of lifeforms are we? All of us
And what's best for each and everyone here?

Flesh

It's imperative we keep flesh intact
We don't want perforations, abrasions
Or undue irritations marring it.
We also want to guard coloration
Of whatever hue hones to its nature,
The smallest capillaries must breathe free.
When a breeze fans it, we love the perk up
When flesh grazes it, we love the perk up
The heat or cold of curiosity.
It's imperative we keep flesh intact.
Painters, if they ever make the comeback
Might plumb flesh, flush out commonality,
Poets, if they ever make the comeback
Might suture flesh, restore integrity.

The Revolution

Gray birds made of marble falling from the sky

Swamp oaks taking two steps forward, if you look closely

Levee water levels rising exactly by four feet

New bridges made of glass suddenly appear over urban canals

Storefront signages swapping places, making sense

Picnics two feet below sea level — in the thousands

Girls with brown eyes rolling boulders into pyramids of gold

Girls with blue eyes casting steel hooks onto silver gates

Girls with green eyes forming a field of grass to skip on

Red, chrome-out chopper cruising the streets, no rider

Purple sun painting twelve windows onto local birthing center

Hell, the word, the concept, scaring no children at this hour

Heaven, the word, the concept, wood cube in dank attic, rotting

Two-minute clip of brawny man battling an alligator in loop mode

One-minute clip of young boy twirling brawny man in loop mode

Sundown western breeze fanning ice tower evaporations

Blank stare of a statue on an iron barge seaward bound

Bats across a full moon portrait in a trash bin flaming

Canoe made of pure sugar gliding over asphalt streets at midnight

Thirty second clip of diamond-toothed baby in loop mode

Bayou bugs onto a fourth generation since yesterday morning

Yellow birds made of polyurethane come to a consensus

Fifteen second clip of upside-down city skyline

Justice, the word, vision, in an orange cloud, distending, glowing

Seven and a half second clip of pencil frolicking on white paper

Four-hundred-foot mound of multicolored masks and panties toppling

Deceased couple with brass canes crossing glass bridge at dawn

Traffic barricades napping again, if you take a glance

The Peopling

AUBADE FOR THE CRESCENT CITY

The 'peopling'
and you gotta
love or hate
that word
of this here
cypress swamp
river bend
is a long long
and super short
complicated
very simple
non-story
of tales
fantastical
voluminous
adding up
to something
while subtractive
of itself
about to
multiply under
the radar
like people's
lived lives
under this here
style of
economic and
cultural dredged
collection of
impulses and

reflexes and
imaginations and
indeed peopling
of people's
peopling
a genuine
non-story
of tales
fantastical
intermittent
fractalled
microns of
feelings and
half thoughts
processed
refined and
marked up
to epic
proportions
dimensions
to get lost in
to meet a few
flakes lost
along the way
showing the way
by tales
fantastical
luminescence
blown away
by raging
storms slammed
against walls of
institutional
administrative

ministerings of
you guessed it
a non-story
of tales
fantastical
interruptive
blown glass
mint julip
fluted beakers
cracking up
spilling out
a micron's
worth of
effect on
the peopling
in process
on boulevards
in alleyways
in sturdy decorative
colorful abodes
and flopping
makeshift tents
under the highway
overpass

Männerbünde

Guns
shedfuls of'em
you'll see
will not be
the deciding factor
in the big shift
towards hemispheric
autarky, no amount
of rounds and clips
hoarded in safes
will rewrite
labor laws that
integrate Canadian
American, and
Mexican bio-power
around a vision
of itself
protective economically
expansive culturally
interposed maps
of watersheds
routes of produce
conduits of
clean energy
lasered in on
healthy work
and stable housing
the big shift
doesn't require
belly crawling
sharpshooters

grown boy camps
männerbünde
singalongs pining
after dreams of
becoming sovereign
when all's entangled
already, except
not formally, and
equitably, set to
a higher order
resource conscious
confident future
commandeering
hemisphere's
collective wealth
material & psychic
brave projection
bulwark against this
anarcho-tyranny
faux nationalism
yacht excursion
for winners of
rigged outcomes
swamp monsters
becoming great again
promoting shedfuls
of ammo, camo
grown up boy
lingerie, boudoir
männerbünde
posing on
towering trucks
performing sovereign
when all's entangled

already, but on
a wobbly base
with sideshows
gun shows
crouching, cowering
last gasps of
sovereign kings
everyman a serf
owning nothing
not mineral deposits
not beds of technology
not downstream planning
educational cargo
material & psychic
oblivious to rising
forces, integrated
autarkic, prosperous
homelands to
thrive in, where
crotch grasping
gun toting
enfeebled copes
flicker out
year by year
as hemispheric power
looks outward
with straight backs
towards other
autarkic regions
working on integration
of a higher order
looking outwards
mindfully negotiating
globe's collective wealth

material & psychic
and yeah, a few
museums of nation-states
and even kinky cosplay
might be entertaining
on occasion
to remind us of
the age of
anarcho-tyranny and its
camo-lingerie'd
butlers on a leash
männerbünde

Beach Time

All y'all:

Alabama flagger flyin'
Cajun dinghy riggin'
Creole beignet flippin'
Texas gravel haulin'
Georgia trailer hitchin'
Mississippi mud draggin'

. . . Gentlemen . . . can we *talk*?

All y'all:

Emerald Coast revelers
Ruby Coast ragers
Sapphire Coast rompers
Pearl Coast plungers
Onyx Coast splashers
Diamond Coast flap abouters

I mean, catch, toss, kick around a bit:

Bent key capitalism
Worn key capitalism
Broken key capitalism
Lost key capitalism
Wrong key capitalism
Keyless fob dead battery capitalism

Not the right time?

I want to agree,
but ripples over there you can see
the white caps of a dark, purple wave
welling up, curling over, sucking in
the water's edge of time
and space
to dream
and drift

Homo Americanus

FREEFORM HOLLERIN' AT THE LIT CONFERENCE (IN SYLLABICS)

1.

No. We don't want you to breathe in — then out.

No need to stand up, stretch out, twirl your wrists.

Most assuredly, no incantations

Are being asked of you, not a single word.

Know what, Jack, Jill? *Scrap* the four directions.

Your identities and ours beside yours

On a coatrack at the door, quite comfy

How much *whacking* can your piñata take?

Yes, you stand on stolen land, you may now

Zounds! Methinks my station merits the ploy

Which, under *these* conditions, is public

Though you're planted on private property.

We do acknowledge *that*: the conditions

The one thousand directions *not to take*

At this after *after* party, we call

Anarcho-Tyranny Über Alles

Or, simply, The Finance Oligarchy.

Please be modest, slithering on the ground

Scooping up treats, subtracting from the whole

Our allotments of failed Liberal Schemes

Coming into view as we splinter up.

2.

Who won the prize? The prize among prizes.

A prize of a prize, you might say, a win

Over one more prize — to win — a prize, won.

Surprise! There's no prize for that. Or for this.

Piñata sticks swung blindly all at once

Is more to the point, bloody point, hobbling

Stumbling onto the arena of Kultur

But what's at a distance tracking it all?

Or, in close: poetics as *detainee*

Marks it a *fugitive* — in mind, and gut.

We were just about to jump outta here

As the smoking debris began to cool

Before the dawn of more Centrist Hokum.

But here we are, herding piss-poor students

Into the bare halls of Career Poet.

There's exactly five things a prize can do:

One: it bestoweth wings to wingless works

Two: it stauncheth today's systemic wounds

Three: perchance it payeth the rent — golly

Four: it groweth wings on the fugitive

Five: it clipeth the fugitive's new wings

3.

Strategies recalibrating tactics

Kind of works. Kind of what might not — is you.

Games abound this side of the barricades

One of them is Self . . . , as *designed* by "you"

But here's another piñata at hand

Popped out from nowhere, perplexing, tempting.

Fellow insurrectionists, lend an ear

Identity thinking stalls <hard reset>

And bullhorn this — all night long, publicly:

Old Universalisms pen us in

Where we mean to run with a New Story.

New Stories, reject Catastrophizing

Refuse a foregone Tragicomedy

Stage an Alternative Futurity

Identity thinking stalls <hard reset>

Blindfolded, Homo Americanus

Grab this trusty stick, grip it mightily

Raise it high — and on the downswing — *crack it*.

Now the bards scramble, now the bards bag up

Scraps of self, whose purpose — *they know not what*

Though it's arousing, all this newfound *pep*.

Brown Lives

Brown lives
the phrase
as is
don't matter
in Mexico
the shades
are endless
where draw
the line
you'd go
quite mad
what matters
in Mexico
is *lana*
cold cash
how much
how far
the flow
what things
what folks
you gather
around you
of course
colorism thrives
in Mexico
weighs in
tips scales
but saying
and insisting
brown lives

the phrase
as is
is sacred
is blurry
happy talk
won't supply
the flow
the things
the folks
you gather
around you
the line
when drawn
would shift
yearly monthly
the haggle
would matter
to oligarchs
a lot
the haggle
would matter
to academia
even more
brown lives
whole departments
might thrive
service lines
blurring oligarchs'
long game
still though
colorism thrives
in Mexico
it hurts
it works

for some
for sure
same families
have winners
and losers
it's important
to confront
colorism frankly
but *lana*
go see
take in
don't flinch
draws lines
on top
down below
both sides
makes box
in Mexico
boxes matter
not lines
that shift
weekly daily
you'd go
quite mad
demarking where
jumping back
jumping over
vying to
drag shit
here to there
and back
stuck in
a box
in Mexico

decaled with
brown lives
matter merch
donated by
happy oligarchs
of oil
of telecom
of finance
beachfront empires
foreground to
hillside slums
background to
nervous middlings
frozen between
undecided about
lines boxes
which matter
and why
earning zeal
spending zeal
to audit
Mexico Lindo
is necessary
the peso
plunging today
ten percent

Barricades

He's fond of peppering in
"on this side of the barricades"
when speaking political
meaning, his critique of
changes at hand
isn't coming from the right
meaning, don't purity spiral
peeps, be stout
allow room for growth
don't be a *gendarme* of
revolution, be a
full actor, unafraid
aware that the barricades
can pop up anywhere
in front *and* back

Iconoclasm

Oh, what's that word, come on
it's like when you, you know
but not exactly — *um*
damn it, I just had it
ah yes! of course, that's it
desecrate (desecrate)
when something that's sacred
gets it bad, *real* bad, as in
"desecrate" "the statue"
like *that*, direct, no bones
which begs — what was sacred?

The Tango

Sometimes
the black/white
tango wears
thin on
the rest

The *tango*
not key
issues
relational
consequential

The tango
you can't
get between
gotta watch
your feet

Again *not*
inflection point
material
potential
for all

But *tango*
white/black
checkerboard
dance floor
all over

Head snapping
stern face
separation
quick embrace
deep dips

Here they *come*
step aside
or — *don't*
grab on
triple tango

Ok here
we *go*
whoa
wait
who's that?

Another?
well alright
ouch
excuse me
this way?

Here we go
full tango
but wait
a new tune's
playing

Marvin Gaye's
"got to *give* it up"
kaleidoscopic
free movement
focus

Unclasp
fingers arms
shoulders hips
chin up
hats off

The Zone

"Panama"
can choose to be
just-Panama
or re-join "Columbia"
in Westphalian 1648
state's sovereignty treaty
legacy modality
or join the Triple Alliance
"Canada" "U.S." "Mexico"
administrative zone
which is a way to say
why "Honduras" now
in this day and age
the region's growing hotter
and hotter crops failing
narcos dominating
new generations which is
a way of saying
"Haiti" at breaking point
won't work as is
folks shriveling there in
zero to scant industry
in need of flotilla
organized and administered
millions out and into
The Zone as with "Guatemala"
sub-administered by
administered "Mexico"
work the pipelines
thousands of aqueducts
water to and fro
like Louisiana rain

to California
Jalisceño blue tequila
to Peoria and Winnipeg
steady work fair work
in The Zone no need
for hideous face tattoos
and special ops
not to mention
failed "Canadian"
nor "American" poets
touting Westphalian
liberal-democratic horizons
cloaked as 'democratic socialism'
socialism — is *para*-national
at the end of the day
private lands allow pipelines
of water to flow
across vast territories
while new train tracks
get laid down eagerly
not self-driving trucks
belching CO^2 and resentment
haulin' veggies and granma
back to town this town
your town's local admin's
intensely responsive
tempered by Northern Zone
general imperatives
takes the wind out of
tiki torch supremacist
carnivals and 'anti-racist'
corporate peddlers in
permanent Westphalian
mode of inclusion into
neoliberal tribalism of
the 1% (actually less)

with same cheery tale
again and again
"American" poets
mute servants to system
quilting idealisms
into patchwork of
safe-spaced silos
border enforcement
at the end of the day
genre and expectation like
is this a legit poem
about "Panama"
or 'global warming'
or the truculence of
sub-sub Westphalian
fatigued nationalism
pickin' and pokin' at
every nook and cranny
of instrumental nostalgic
Best American _____
Best Canadian _____
Best Mexican _____
empirical mass ornament
gray verses sung to
scratchy music score of
b-movie for *inter*
(Westphalian) nationalism's
finance driven identities
plus sub-sub identities
dragooned by
Anarcho-Tyranny as
that is *the deal*
before the establishment
and careful conducting of
The Zone

Jump-Start Poems

I wonder, too, if jump-start poems are worth it

I mean, poems, meant to get at existential being itself

For a moment (brief moment) stripped of social causality

Not having to take a publicly recognizable position

Not having to, you know, massage an affiliation

But instead, riffing on what's elementally human

What's fundamentally common *between* folks

Instead of *about* folks, as proclaimed by folks

Jump-start poetry that pivots around a few key words

Words that, for the moment (brief moment) hold the mystery

The puzzle of being in time on this planet

Or not even being on this planet, but wanting to

I wonder if jump-start poems are a cop out

Or a necessary moment (brief moment) against cop out

Or maybe something in between — stuck, broken

I wonder if folks are almost always in between

Copping out, not copping out, copping out, not copping out

But play it like they're one or the other, certain

I wonder if jump-start poems even exist

And if they don't, whether they *should* exist

You know, poems that pivot around certain words

Words, like "being" "folks" "mystery" "pivot"

And if they do exist, whether they wonder themselves

About poems that wonder about *not* wondering

Fending off the hounds of lassitude, indolence, and surrender

Just long enough for a jump-poem to start it all

Compulsory Conviction

Many these days demand a show of faith
Oblations on the altar of justice
Rounding up neophytes, exhaling charms
Cooked up by professional spell casters.
There's others though that need a space to think
Step back and stoke the embers of feeling
Matching sensing to thinking, cell by cell
Tender shoots of enlightenment spring free.
There's some these days that don't need poetry
Or think they don't, costumed in starchy tweets
Surveying the field of battle with pride
Everyone an instant Napolean.
When strengthening shoots harden into trunks
Roots twist into action, upturn church walls.

Ally

Splatter your door with the blood of a lamb
And spare yourself the fury of Yahweh
And while you're at it, declare *ally-ship*
A week before your yacht cruise in Cape Cod
Month after deceased dad's condo transfer
Twenty years before your daughter rebels
Calls you out on shit waiting for coin drop
Deposit from gramp's magic box of wit
Keep the wages sensibly low golf club
Hitting the course your brother tweets out blood
Cousin affirms, genuflects, steps off yacht
He's not a *true* ally sister affirms
In the reconstructive doc's recliner
Slyly rubbing one out before the blade

Compeers

No poems for compeers in your work world
For at least six months, more often, longer.
Poetry, movement poetry, more so
Captures contradiction, not punditry.
Whatever the motion one's adding to
If it's not zig-zagging, it's not alive.
Those that rah-rah their way become rearguard
At the end of the day, vanguard poets
Turn into double oppositionists
That is, friends to those that refuel the fight
Tackle orthodoxics, defrocking pride
Risking oneself to play the heretic.
When compeers learn the contours of your heart
Send them some poems in timely doses.

Blank Page
AKA WORLD OPINION

O blank page you *flub* — welcome

Splattered DNA of societies to come

Come — dangle ideologic dongs, tits, balls

Post-material *puss* for abstract neuter cum dried up on meta belly to *be* that

Or whatever scramble y'all prefer

Or whatever scramble y'all prefer

There was a feisty court of *world opinion*

Where the battle lay between Global and The Interiorites

The Live Anywheres vs. The Live Hereabouters

Yokels — step up — be stout

Trotters — tread lightly — grip tight

The jingles — got'em?

So you got a Ukrainian Nationalist Berliner bent on Non-Russo-Zone Narratives — *catch*

So you got a Russian Trans-Nationalist bent on Transducing U.S. Regional Tensions — *catch*

More to come

The count — ready?

Zero Non-Academic in Poetry Journal

Zero Construction Sector Folks

Zero Service Sector Folks

Zero Maritime Sector Folks

Zero Agricultural Sector Folks

Zero Domestic Work Sector Folks

Zero Medical Sector Folks

Alarms 1 through 7

The jingles

And you got an Americanist bent on Transliterating an Atlanticist Cultural Command Center — *release*

And you got a Bi-Continental Futurologist bent on Boiling Down World Pop Culture as Failed Local Folk Ways — *release*

Count'em up — splash hydrochloric acid on it

Deep Burn on the Brawny Brain of World Siblinghood

Count'em up — peel off the mask

O Blank Page! miss you

Societal DNA — *nobody* knows it

O but for clues!

You got a Chinese F-1 Visa Fellow bent on 1990's PRC Deep-Encrypted Resistance Poetry — *catch*

And you got a (*never* forget U.K. twisted legacy regional mapping) Kurdish Cultural Operative bent on Dark Web Podcast Scene Shake Up — *catch*

So what's the count — now?

Alarm 8

There *is* no truce between Communitarians and Individualists — *as yet*

Scramble (it) (it) (it) (it) (it)

Splattered DNA of the Dying Society of Forgotten Motives on the Move

Finance Sector Bowling Ball towards your teeth — clench, *absorb*

DNA of Decomposing Aesthetic Solutions to Everyday Capitalist Time Strictures Implemented As: Games

Countem' up — portside / starboard

Over-representation of Incubating Northeastern Mass Urbanites Apportioning National Aesthetic Pills — *release*

Over-representation of the Evolving Lords of Devolving Education Departmentalism — *release*

The jingles

Jingle jingle little square, trapezoidal   in   a   *hole*

And you got a Bay Area Canadian bent on — Bay Area Canadianism — *lottery draw*

And you got a (remember the cosmos — always) Chicano Disco Ball
Erotic Poet bent on Social Justice — *lottery draw*

Or whatever scramble y'all prefer

The ship hole — *what*?

The hole in the ship! *oh*

Where the battle they said was between The *Urbs* and the Sub-*Urbs*

The Taste Anythings vs. The Tried N' Truers

And what the devil does "transducing" mean?

And what about "transliterating"?

Ship ahoy!

Communitarians — bent on deck chair rearrangement — portside

Individualists — bent on deck chair *cushions* rearrangement — starboard

Alarms 9 & 10

Zero Former or Current Military Sector

Zero Informal Paid Sex Sector

Alarm 11

Zero Energy Extraction and Distribution Sector

Scramble it   Zero + Zero + Zero

And   if you relate well with people — and are *fair* and *balanced* (but not
"most watched")

You're a Same Ole!

Hurray for Same Ole!
Same Ole! *Same Ole*! *Same Ole*! *Same Ole*!

Those for equal sign — *same*

Rapid Thaw in the Grassy Brain of World Siblinghood

Hereabouters pumped about Symbolic Saviorship — T-Man
dosed / T-Man duped — *catch*

Anywherers pumped about Symbolic *Contra*-Saviorship —
T-Man dosed / T-Man duped — *catch*

Same Oles — gathering mass

Indivisible   Zero + Zero + Zero + Zero + Zero

Jingle jingle little   hole   "hi"

And you got a Dual   Citizen   *ghost*   making you lunch

And you got a Mono   Citizen   *precariat*   serving you lunch

Ship ahoy!

What scramble — y'all prefer?

Zeros — on the move — Same Ole

Globals and Interiorites — step lively — *off* deck

Rapid Re-Freeze over the Watery Brain of World Siblinghood

My *glory*!   someone spouts   Spare Us

My *lord*!   someone blurts   Bring It On

Scramble (it) (it) (it) (it) (it)

The jingles

Damn right I got'em!

Blank Page — *fuckin'*— pick up your shit and get movin'

Orphan Poem

This poem
is a poem
without a project

Like those dreams
of you naked
in public

Where to hide
where's my underwear
can they see me

This poem
is a poem
without a sponsor

Like a refugee
we gawk at
on television

How far the shore
where the patrols
when the rescue

This poem
is a poem
without an identity

Like a stray
along a fence line
before a storm

When's the next meal
where's the next nap
  — that a *friend* or *foe*?

Pandemic

The end of this, that, the other
All anyone's thinking or says

How about an intermission?
Slight rattle, stir, curtain opens

Percussion grenade lands on stage
Soft-shoe routine done in silence

Firing mechanism funks out
Slight rattle, stir, curtain closes

Great anticipation . . . hold tight
Tittering starts, curtain opens

Carnival barker hops on stage
Slams cane to floor for tempo

Soft-shoe routine done in silence
Percussion grenade shell spinning

Dire Straights

By now, affairs in offices
have cooled down; some, surely
have heated up, and millions
will never see the light of day

By now, the gene sorting machine
office towers at noon
are empty of their shadow purpose
as the sun softly sets

What is not a sheer collision
in human affairs?
What location is safe
from lust, love, and loss?

Clarity

The world of women
is ending, as is
the world of men
children's worlds
are on the wane too
animals still thrive
though, to us, they are
quite done, as is the sky
and the oceans too
fading from view
along with the stars
long gone, the moon
was the first to go
and amazingly, the sun
went with it, gone
are grasses, to us
meadows murmur
in utter darkness
forests are forgotten
houses, neighborhoods
cities and nations
poof — gone
the arts, humanities
fond fountains of hope
flaming out, as are
'critiques of power'
'interstitial freedoms'
smoky afterglow, ash
music, of all things
remains, is unfazed

by this psychodrama
of absence, disappearance
and dance is — a hop away
science, what remains of it
is like the animals
unruffled, and *in it*
the whole bloody way

Nowhereville

First words, top o' the morn, wet towel slap
To the face: 'Two aircraft carriers race
To the South China Sea', to what degree
Allow your first thoughts to be commandeered
Navigating to nowhereville, surely
Your trusty app can avail *other* words:
'U.S. quits World Health Organization'
Fresh slap to the nards or cooch — *oopsie do*
An app called Total Slap — nine ninety-nine
In nowhereville goes for *three ninety-nine*
'Provides ready relief for minor burns'
Sends daily, top o' the morn, pep pills, like:
'Two carriers to the South China Sea
Pay no mind, *grill*, you jus' wanna grill, bro'

Thing & Thang

Is the U.S. a nation
or just an economic platform?
because, a nation, is (or can be)
an expression of its people.

Platforms, as you know
support a ton of apps
but not all, and often
not many at all.

Nations, of course, excel at
spinning origin stories that
somewhat stick, actually
too often, stick, too long.

These days, folks, are *sick*
of platforms, they feel
but more than that, *know*
the grift and graft.

But also, folks, can't won't
booty hop for nation
not for the past, nor future
and for damn sure, not now.

Alright, *some* are nation
afterschool drama types
never miss a chance to flame
in public, funk out, in private.

Others are *pure* platform
all day trendsetters
brahmins, actually, prancing like
Jack & Jill nobodies.

Yet others, in idealist mode
strain to marry the two
nation thing & platform thang
triangle into circle slot.

Problem is, Globo Bobo's diet
consists of broken idols
shards of meritocracies
the bootstrap's scraps.

Platform thang, over amped
promises a commonwealth of
continuous profile updates
hexagons into pentagonal slots.

Nation thing, flustered
promises to calm anxieties
save selves from intermixing
in golden wheat fields swaying.

Globo Bobo, or if you prefer
Bobo Globo, plays it safe
defers to neither Thing nor Thang
but tabulates and waits.

GB, might well be
progressive *or* regressive
no one can say for now
poltergeist inside us.

Huddle

A REVERIE ON ANTECOVIDUM SOIRÉES

Mix it up
make it count
delight folks
be delighted
steer phrases
be steered
in the swirl
roust about
seek a huddle
spot a huddle
slink in
stick out
seek gaps
shoot them
spot walls
crash them
step back
make space
watch huddle
sidebar one
slip a shiny
receive well

what rebounds
pocket insight
pocket wit
move on
in the swirl
seek a huddle
spot a huddle
slink in
say nothing
nod a bit
make it count
seek a signal
spot a signal
drop a shiny
kick it once
kick it twice
kick it thrice
scoop it up
toss it
receive well
what rebounds
step back
make space
watch huddle
empty pockets

show empty
share empty
fill empty
with shinies
kicked around
from nowhere
to somewhere

Zoom Reader

Square 1, if you insist on knowing
has fucked squares 3, 6, and 14

Square 2, not too hard to imagine
also fucked square 3, plus 5 and 9

Square 8, according to square 13
will soon be fucking square 5

Square 4 — who could have guessed it
took a hard pass on fucking square 1

Square 5, we somehow know
fucked square 11 and 12 — at once

Square 6, when factoring out variables
has fucked no square, but beware

Square 7, you can't not *not* tell us
hasn't fucked square 2

Square 8 (blacked out), I intuit (again)
is fucking square 10 (blacked out)

Square 9, everybody knows
is bent on fucking square 4, *after* 3

Square 10, we can extrapolate
would *un*-fuck square 13, if possible

Square 11, according to the algorithm
might well fuck square 6, and soon

Square 12 (in speaker mode) drops a hint
it fucked square 7 (on mute)

Square 13 (the host) just won't tell
if square 5 might fuck me, oh well

Square 14, we've come to a consensus
has been fucking itself, poker faced

Quitters

Band of about 14
quitters, roaming about

done quit boards
and editorialships

demanded someone quit
but quit themselves

in this State of Quit
14 roam about

two quitting over
two others having not

and of the two
now roaming about

one demands the other
quit now or else

split on who quit first
the charge being *false quit*

meanwhile, band of 12
split over roaming

6 quit on the spot
over six not quitting

so now 6 are roaming
and 6 are not roaming

the non-roamers
split over banding itself

the roam-abouters
split over splitting itself

one from each band
calls it quits on the fly

they meet, begin roaming
seeking The Big Join

they meet a stray
former quit leader

they form a roaming band
declaring quit *forbidden*

former leader sneaks off
at midnight, a stray

stray roams about
feeling a split inside

half that stray now
seeking The Big Join

half that stray now
seeking The Big Quit

Latinx Poet

Sometimes X leans Tang Dynasty
and is glad to tell these Romans
who've stuck around for the last call
chumming it with Delta Blues Folk
razzing Elizabethan bards

Says X, "Ahoy Futurist brutes
on seven stages vogueing to
Post-LangPo cell group epsilon
in harmonic consonance with
3rd wave Xicano *presente*"

And what do they say these Romans
to X wobbling on a bar stool
pensive about collapsing towards
Infrarealists moshing with
Canadian Kootenay Kool Dub?

"3rd wave Harlem Renaissancing
bouncing to Symbolist techno
with acoustic Marxist *lehrstuck*
at Baroque toccata tempi
is true NOLA line strutting *yo*"

And X, supine retorts skyward
just as the Beat Front rounds the curb
sighting the tail end of ConPo
clearing the path for gen-u-wine
Ruskie Constructivism "*yeah*"

To which these Romans saucily
counterpoint to drop precisely
"do all-night donk to donk with *Gronk*
skanking it up to cop a feel
Castilian Lit pre-1610"

Mundus

Let's have a look at the world in seconds
Not by what you're being told, as I'm being told
Let's do a little tech check, see what's wonky
Locally, yeah, globally, for decades
We called for regional dependency
And got a sloppy joe of nation state
We called for superconductive labor
Across cubicles and vibrant valleys
Not to mention industrial sink holes
"Here goes the project on course in due time
Here go the nights of leisure and dreaming"
Let's have a look at the world, day by day
They send us an invoice for self-image
We transfer currencies of disbelief

Eye of the Storm

You don't want a plane crash in your backyard
To wake you up to matter, its contours
Same for sound, if sound's grown that dull to you
Not to mention smell: no need for plane crash
If your imagination's running dry
Or if you need a sense of urgency
Or an event to help you spin a tale
A plane crash is something that's way too much
Like a voter suppressed fall election
Springing everybody into action
Unmooring sensuous life in its path
And despite the odds being fifty-fifty
A serene hole in the sky opening
You venture this speck of time to say: *no*

Coconuts

You said, "what's missing here is coconuts"
In a handstand on the hood of your car
In a crowded shopping mall parking lot
In the long summer of twenty twenty
Buck naked, rainbow against a black sky
Eyes side to side, straining a focused grin
"What's missing here is coconuts" and then
You jumped on the roof of your car, arms wide
Pissing while reciting a hundred times
"Payroll tax cut now? Pay full sum later?
But if we vote you in, sum forgiven?"
And as the mall patrol was approaching
You slinked into a sort of shark outfit
Thrashing off like a senator beach pimp

The Mounds

Tips of spears, pottery shards, how bones lay
Shell's beach of origin, which way stones point
Mounds not clear to the eyes at first, rising
Kinda mushy (by now) generations
Of grass, of ceaseless rain, blurring the lines
Of forethought, persistence, endurance, wit
Rendering the scene (truth be told) vacant
To eyes and ears tethered to blinking screens
Superstructures driving your sex by bits
You think it was different back in the day?
Smoky campfires, come gather round, listen
Hear those that came before, left all this junk
As we fast ditch *our* junk, dreaming deep space
Always deep space is sex as skulls retrieved

Destinations of Things

Consumables, ponder them briefly, *breathe*
Circuit board mound, forty meters in height
Jakarta slum, pickers climb high to pluck
Teeny, tiny chips, *there*, there's a one, *breathe*
Exhale, what's stirring behind the curtain?
What's rattling there? Bring on the chronicler!
Eighty ten kilo buckets in a row
The clunking's increasing, now fading . . . gone
Shsh . . . is that a one? It's back! Supply line
Tankards! tankards! bring on the sorcerer!
Oh you mother plucker son of a bit!
Breathe, it's calling out, tankards, supply lines
Bring on the rhapsodist! Buckets, *exhale*
This micro play of words as chips in play

Write The City

What's the point of New York City
Or, for that matter, Calgary
Or any city on a hill
Or hidden far beneath the waves
Any city at any time
Any city planned or dreamt of

What's the point of males and females
What's the rub with transportation
Movement of foodstuffs or the arts
Distribution of new pleasures
Or the same old ones, year by year
Making for a steady story

What's the point of stock characters
Emotions bundled or spread out
Arguments over arguments
Escapes from argumentation
Fantastical propositions
Promises to extend a hand

What's the point of scheduling things
All in tandem or at random
Through avenues, streets, and alleys
Secrets secreted forever
Or spilled onto morning pavement
Draining into holes seaward bound

What's the point of that lingerie
That tie's length & width, and color
Fraying from overuse or disuse
Weighing x-amount per square ton
Legs, rubber, arms, cotton, eyes, steel
What point in writing the city

1519 Aztec Arrivista

"I want to make sure to register my full support for Zapotec Power
With respects to Mixtec Power, derived from Toltec Power
Transposed from Mayan Power, indebted to Totonac Power
Taking a page from Olmec Power
When given the chance to validate Tarascan Power in the Present
And defer to the rising Chichimec Power
In alliance with the Cholulan Complex
Six hundred years of illicit Serpentine Sex
Atop the Teotihuatecan Simplex"

Clouds and Us

Can't believe clouds
are on center stage
again, bloviations
how clouds shape up
and stretch, make faces
puff up, darken
and pee softly
or raucously
friggin clouds
meaning *everything*
to hungry ancients of
five minutes ago
mixed chalk with oil
twirling brushes
making clouds talk
sock puppets
for dreams and hopes
of *healthy* clouds
as if sick ones
could even be
here's a set of four
ok, now three
make that five
clouds, we can agree
are non-numerical
neither the Dow Jones
nor S&P 500
tracks'em trades'em
nobody squawks about
breakdown of

cloud families
nor about clouds
going back to school
we can all agree
no jobs for clouds
unconscious drifters
Wordsworth wrote
"I wandered lonely
as a cloud," well
that's closing in
on the matter
the will to flee
but not quite like
"I floundered
antsy as a
socialist geek
putting clouds
on center stage
for future ancients
to riff off
same mists
distending to nowhere
meaning *everything*
from drinking
to cooking
to bathing
to *bottling* — ok!
guess clouds *are*
tracked n' traded
somewhat like

human labor
accrues steadily
hinting that
some kind of
cross-entity
solidarity arises
tween clouds and us
demanding tribute
and ritual, like
the scary gods
of yore"

July 4th, 2020

Two words
per line
quite skimpy
but plenty
for nation
to summon
half inflated
rubber raft
collecting dust
under house

Sparkling bayou
stone's throw
invites revelry
to come
float about
meander again
minute moments
ahead demand
fetch raft
find pump

Can do
ice chest
can do
beer cans
can do
skeeter spray
might can
well do

fireworks launch
covid forgot
Two words
per line
creep slow
to flow
with gators
down below
other realms
grinding on
crack can
cheers ahoy

Can do
chipper talk
can do
nation pause
can do
play today
if moved
to drag
dusty raft
to shore

Sparkling bayou
raining cinders
flaming sky
infections high
raft adrift
amid rafts
adrift amid
rowing dreams
wake to
crackling hiss

Chillaxer

Ticonderoga "warrior" pencil
Veltin's pilsner, product of Germany
Six by eleven hardbound black sketch pad
Mississippi river bend — barges, smoke
Blinding sun at dusk, dragonflies, lone man
Frolickers toss Frisbee, mosquito meal
Flowering hazelnut, piss place supreme
Folding chair for gramps, product of China
Cheery, chitter, chatter, tugboat horn blare
Foucault looking fellow, red shades, strumming
Young mom's wooden beads, product of Tonga
Couple shuffling through tote, something lost, found
A fisherman — when not — a fisherman
Booties, of course, everywhere, urging on

The Buzz

The moon is
probably not quiet
likely has a buzz
of its own
we can't hear it
and if we could
wouldn't understand
still, it'd be
nice to hear
from the moon
once in a while
you know
add contrast to
sun's buzz
and of course
the stars abuzz
which, for now
might be
who knows
something else's
should we say
music, or just
buzz, wasn't that
a 70's word
"buzz," we forget
was it, "what's
the buzz, yo?"
or, "buzzin' hard
are you, mate?"
or, "what's buzzin'?"

— that's it
what's buzzin'
well, who the hell
you know
can say
most things
individual things
if "individual"
is a thing
kind of don't say
shit — ever
and what if
the moon's been
serenading *us*
jokc's on us
lute in hand
feathered hat, or
slide steel
badass
crooning
till the sun's up
and says
what's buzzin', y'all?
while we say
what's buzzin', y'all?

Mysterium

The Big Outside, the Deepest Internal
And zone that's imagined between the two
Intermundia, where energies meet
All that kind of cackle is diverting
From the higher realm that's neither concrete
Nor an abstraction seeking a concrete
Rather, it's a field that's fast unfolding
Not *in* time, nor *of* space, but both as one
A vantage point of no point of vantage
Grand fluidity as yet without name
Containing all words everywhere at once
Though the dire illusion of word by word
Makes for poems able to stand and walk
As we sit in boredom, wonder, or glee

Ape or Ant

I study my hand, and I know I'm ape
On top of that, or under, there's an ant
Spastic, every which way, quite familiar
Maniacally, being all it can be — ant
To add a dash of drama to the scene
A termite's drag racing on the table
As the value of labor's in free fall
Outside, here, in a half-shut brewery
Termite crosses finish line — is devoured
Surely, time for another pint — to go
But stay, like ants, guarding the colony
An allotment of space in time, in mind
Among three hundred thirty million apes
Think they're gods, ever awake, with a plan

Litigators

He gets up there and — yeah, another litigant

Love that litigant — or, maybe not — *write the*

Next! next litigant — bring on the

Here — lemme litigate — a tad

Litigational — *that's* the quality we're looking for

Floats — giant swans — flotillas — on still waters

Music from a giant conch shell

Don't feed the litigators

Y'all assin' it to a seat — or — propped up on feat

Don't feed the litigators

Snout — peeking up — from the swamp — couple dragonflies — floozy

What else fits the portrait?

You wake up — peek at the news

You go to bed — peek at the news

Daytime swamp touring — you guessed it

WHEN YOU DIE

There'll be litigation — some — ok — barely

You got on a plane — you checked into your room

You're prepping — hoping — dreaming — scheming

Cute litigators

Stressed out, easy breezy, brainiac

Snout — cruisin — cruisin — cruisin

YEAH OK — you fuck — you *fuck* folks — you fuck *folks* — then what?

Cruisin'

Litigational cruises limited liability for-profit national program security clearance protocol

Floats — fireworks — strings in unison — rising from a conch shell

Li'l dragonfly round the — *is fed*

You eat what's fed you?

Next up we have

Let's give it up for

It's a *dream* — come true

We're *so* excited

Snout

Moonlight

Conch shell

Float

Music — imperial — enigmatic

A night of

A summer of

A lifetime of

You take a break — and *on* your break

Yup

LITIGATE

Silently performatively

WHEN YOU'RE BORN

You're dying already

Buffo — WHAT A RELIEF

Magma

Top *magma*

You wanna be top dog?

Top magma

Top magma on the move

To enigmatic music

Assin' it to a seat — or propped up on feet

Snout — see it?

Next up

The quality we're looking for

Prepped

Cruisin'

You wake up — *bang* — face ripped off

News peeking in

Litigate *that*

Quietly — profoundly — loudly — perfunctorily

Wretch — LITIGATE — now

Cloud covers moon — cloud moves aside

MOONLIGHT

Giant conch shell — floats — kettle drums — woodwinds

Moonlit snouts

Swamp tours

Journals, anthologies, prizes

Swamp tours

Magma

Strings in unison

Imperial beat

Dreams/schemes — schemes/dreams

THE EXCEPTION

She gets up there and yeah, another litigant

LOVE that litigant — or — maybe not — *write the*

Next — bring on the

Climbing onto the float like that — chomping at the conch

MOONLIGHT

Or — prepping for moonlight — you know

Litigate to *prep* for moonlight

THE EXCEPTION

Angelic Body

Floating — gliding alongside

Nobody knows it

Everybody wants it

The litigators are:

Magma

Cruisin'

Prepped

Next up:

Angelic Body

Floating — gliding alongside

Nobody knows it

Everybody wants it

The litigators are:

Dragonflies

Moon

Drums

Snouts — see them?

Broke Folks Poem

Get a word in, edgewise, before
Gronk has its way
is still the challenge

Gronk — is a stand-in for society
To get a move on is tough
weaving through words

What counts for "our word"
is limited and bartered
at times, it's illicit

Chasing down *Gronk* all day
gets you a space program
and a cheapie patch of grass

Some words get in, edgewise
other words simply give up
without a bullhorn at hand

Universal Basic Income

One third of This City
is on fritz, on the bubble
on the chopping block

Sapiens nowhere to turn
Sapiens imploding and yeah
Sapiens about to burst — *bang*

To hell with — who can't see it
To hell with — who don't face it
To hell with — who won't fix it

Two thirds of This City
On an island, or a lucky yacht
Waving to the shore, chipper

Still, one third of This City
on the injured list, out to pasture
in lines — *on*-line — endless hours

Sapiens behind the eight ball
Sapiens patient, for the most part
Sapiens done *done* with band aids

Feel-Serf

For sure, I'm often piss and vinegar
Some might think something's deeply missing here
Some might be totally right — I don't care
Who cares if *I'm* right about *your* cope schemes?
No one, or few, care about you *or* me
But *something* has its laser on us all
It's a surveillance society this one
It's both personal and ultra-public
It's a great center without being centered
It's a margin without edging the rim
It's full Anarcho-Tyranny, confreres
The fees on your hospital bills are tithes
To this fiefdom of privatization
Where *options* to be a *feel-serf* — are free.

Englisc

Done
with you
for the time being
bayou's ducks
in creole French
back and forth
in Castilian
laid off cooks
in Tagalog
at water's edge
in Celtic
stifling humidity
in Vietnamese
stifling prospects
in German
construction continues
in Mandarin
ducks paddling by
in Neapolitan
back and forth
in Nigerian
minimal ambulance howl
in Greek
Porsche flies by
in Punjabi
homeless placard flaps
in Romanian
back and forth
in Bantu
teens in jeeps

in Persian
picnickers gather
in Hebrew
ducks bobbing
in Malaysian
invisible 4g pulse
in Norwegian
three f-15's streaking
in Korean
back and forth
in Somali
reeds random swaying
in Arabic
ducks take flight
in Russian
beers cans snapping
in Chitimacha
dark clouds gathering
in Houma
bayou clearing
in Choctaw

Socialist War Plan

She was *sorta* in school, *sorta* living at home
sorta making money, *sorta* dating

Sorta scribbling things

One day, she declared herself a general

The campaign required a van, a Gulf Coast interstate
a thousand dollars a month (every month)
a bundle of twenty books (two of them, notebooks)
a slew of talkative strangers

serene moonlight

rye whiskey

Converse

A REVOLUTIONARY PROGRAM FOR TOTAL CHANGE

To say something
then something else

To be still, waiting
to comprehend

To help out
being helped by others

To make stuff
in tandem

To rip asunder
the making

To point very far
feeling it close

To pull the screen up
and laugh

Working The Room

Energy
smooth operator of the universe
lighting up stars that burst
                              coalesces
into a clump of carbon
                       speaking

I should say something
in this room
Why I'll tell you something
in this room
(think of the biosphere as a room)

Poems greedily suck energy from the room

and expend it on the spot

(there
        energy having it's greedy say

in a generous way)